BEVERLEY:

A STROLL THROUGH TWELVE CENTURIES

by

PAMELA HOPKINS

Illustrated by Jenny Francis

HUTTON PRESS

1987

Published by the Hutton Press Ltd.
130 Canada Drive, Cherry Burton, Beverley
East Yorkshire HU17 7SB

Published 1987
Reprinted 1988, 1989, 1990
Reprinted 1991, 1993

Printed by Clifford Ward & Co.
(Bridlington) Ltd.
55 West Street, Bridlington, East Yorkshire
YO15 3DZ

ISBN 0 907033 53 9

Introduction

From whichever direction you approach Beverley, the two towers of the Minster dominate the scene. For the last 500 years they have acted as beacons to travellers, guiding them on to the ancient market town of Beverlac, which means beaver clearing in the wood.

Travelling on the A1079 from York, you will cross the Westwood, one of the pastures on which freemen of Beverley had the right to pasture cattle. Often on a cloudy day the sunlight will shine on the towers of the Minster and St. Mary's Church, making these two buildings stand out from the rest of the town.

Yet the history of the town goes back for 500 years before the building of these churches began. It is an interesting history, for although Beverley may appear to be far from the centre of events, every development of the English people seems to be reflected in the history of this town.

CHRONOLOGY OF BEVERLEY

719		Bishop John of York retired to Beverley
721		John of Beverley died
787	First invasion of the Norsemen	
867	Viking Kingdom of York	Minster destroyed by Viking Raid
938		King Athelstan grants right of sanctuary to Beverley; established a Collegiate Church
1035	Final end of Danish rule	
1037		John of Beverley made a saint
1066	William conquers England	
1120		Building of St. Mary's begins
1188		Fire in Beverley destroys many houses
1201		Manor given to Knights Hospitallers
1213		Central tower of Minster collapses
1220		Building of present Minster begins
		Edward I visits Beverley
1299		Market established every Wednesday/Saturday
1300-10		Edward I and II visit Beverley on many occasions
1328		Percy tomb built
1349	Black Death — third of population dies	
1377		Poll tax shows Beverley to be 11th largest town in England
1388		Westwood given to the people of Beverley
1408		Henry IV visits Beverley
1409		North Bar built
1420		Building of Minster completed
1535	Archbishop Fisher (born in Beverley) executed	
1536	Henry dissolves monasteries	Pilgrimage of Grace
1540		Right of Sanctuary curtailed
1588	Defeat of Spanish Armada	
1642	Civil War	King Charles at Beverley
1643		John Hotham executed
1649	King Charles beheaded	
1660	End of Commonwealth	
1714		Market Cross completed
1778		North Bar Without planned
1793	War with France	
1799		William Crosskill born
1804		Playhouse in Lairgate
1846		Railway opened in Beverley
1860		New Workhouse built — now Westwood Hospital
1866		New Cattle Market built
1868		Bribery at elections
1886		Corn Exchange built
1901		Cook shipyard established
1913		Armstrong built own car
1914	World War I	
1918		Much building after war
1939	World War II	
1974		Humberside County Council established headquarters in Beverley

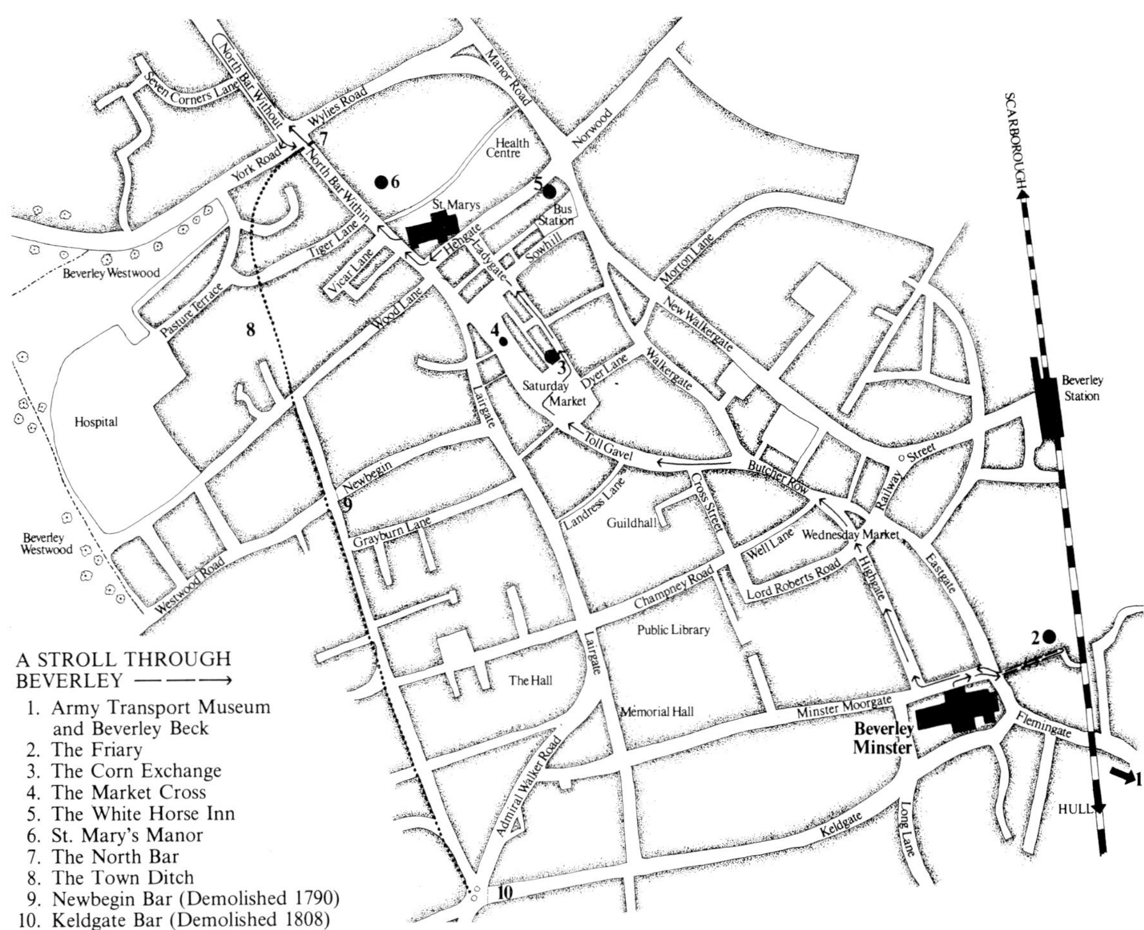

A STROLL THROUGH BEVERLEY
1. Army Transport Museum and Beverley Beck
2. The Friary
3. The Corn Exchange
4. The Market Cross
5. The White Horse Inn
6. St. Mary's Manor
7. The North Bar
8. The Town Ditch
9. Newbegin Bar (Demolished 1790)
10. Keldgate Bar (Demolished 1808)
Seven Corners Lane
North Bar Without
Wylies Road
Manor Road
Norwood
York Road
North Bar Within
Health Centre
St. Marys
Bus Station
Hengate
Ladygate
Sowhill
Tiger Lane
Vicar Lane
Wood Lane
Beverley Westwood
Pasture Terrace
Hospital
Morton Lane
New Walkergate
Walkergate
Dyer Lane
Saturday Market
Lairgate
Toll Gavel
Butcher Row
Newbegin
Grayburn Lane
Landress Lane
Guildhall
Cross Street
Well Lane
Wednesday Market
Lord Roberts Road
Highgate
Champney Road
Public Library
Westwood Road
The Hall
Memorial Hall
Minster Moorgate
Beverley Minster
Flemingate
Eastgate
Railway Street
Beverley Station
SCARBOROUGH
HULL
Admiral Walker Road
Keldgate
Long Lane

View of the Bar from North Bar Without. An imposing entrance to the town.

Origins of the Town of Beverley

The history of the town begins with the story of St. John of Beverley. Although there is no actual proof that he actually came to this area, the story is that in 719 John, Bishop of York, retired and came to live in a small wooden monastery in a clearing in a wood, the site of the present Minster.

During his life he was said to be a saintly man, and performed many miracles. Some of his miracles are recorded for us in the Venerable Bede's *History of the English Church and People.* One such miracle was when John went to dedicate the church of the Thane Puch. This church is believed to have been on the site of the present church at Bishop Burton. Puch's wife had been ill for 40 days and for three weeks it had been impossible to move her. After dedicating the church, John was persuaded by Puch and Berthun (John's deacon), after promising to give alms to the poor, to delay the two-mile return journey to his monastery at Beverley and dine with Puch in his house. John sent one of his monks to give Puch's wife some of the dedicated water from the church. She was to drink a little of it and some was to be laid upon the affected area of her body. The woman was immediately cured and felt strong enough to spend the rest of the evening serving drinks to her husband and friends.

When John died in 721 his bones were kept in a casket in the small monastery he had founded. Pilgrims came from afar to worship at the shrine of this holy man and in 1037 he was made a saint.

Consequently, Beverley became an important religious centre and a small community developed here. Evidence of Saxon buildings has been found in the field to the south of the Minster. The wooden monastery was probably destroyed in 861 when Viking invaders came to plunder the riches of the churches.

The Vikings settled in this area and for 150 years were the rulers of this part of England with their capital in York. Evidence of their stay in Beverley is reflected in the names of the streets. The Viking word for street was 'gate' and many of Beverley's streets end with this word, e.g. Lairgate, Hengate, Highgate, etc.

The importance of Beverley as a religious centre remained and in 934 King Athelstan, first overlord of Britain and grandson of Alfred the Great, visited the shrine of John, making a detour on his way to fight with the Scots at Brunanberg. (The actual site of this battle is unknown.) He visited this holy church and, leaving his dagger on the altar, vowed that if successful in battle he would return.

Luckily for Beverley he was successful, and in 938 returned to fulfil his vow. He is also reputed to have granted certain rights to the town:

> To have given the Minster the status of a collegiate church (i.e. to have regular secular priests called canons, ruled by a provost).

Statue in the Minster of King Athelstan who granted certain rights to the town.

To have endowed the church with lands.

To have allowed the town of Beverley to be exempt from paying tax. (Alas, this exemption no longer operates!)

To have granted the town the right of sanctuary.

The Right of Sanctuary

On three approaches to Beverley — the A164 from Hull, the B1230 from Walkington and the A1079 from York — the observant traveller will notice an upright stone on the side of the road approximately one mile from the Minster. These are known as Sanctuary Stones.

For nearly 600 years — between 938 and 1540 — any

A Saxon Sanctuary Stone on the road from Beverley to York.

person believed to have committed an offence and escaping from his pursuers, could claim the Right of the Sanctuary of the Minster. If captured once he had passed one of these stones, the pursuers had to pay a fine of approximately £8. If captured at the Minster door, the fine was increased to £96 and if at the altar, £144. A rich man indeed who could afford such a fine. He was also liable to be excommunicated by the church.

Once in the Minster, the fugitive would be looked after by the canons for 30 days. In return he would promise not to wear a dagger, put out fires in the town, help quell riots and assist with the mass.

During his 30 days of protection, the canons of the Minster would investigate the fugitive's crime, and if found guilty he would be escorted to the coast and put on a ship to the continent. If found innocent, he would be free to go where he liked, and many such fugitives chose to remain in the prosperous town of Beverley.

View from Highgate looking towards the Minster. It was from the room above the porch of the north door of the Minster that the priest would watch the fugitive coming down Highgate (then Londoner Street) to claim the Sanctuary of the Minster.

The Building of the Minster

On the 20th September 1188, much of the town of Beverley was burnt, together with the noble church of Blessed John the Archbishop. The church was restored after the fire, but in 1213 disaster struck again when the newly erected tower collapsed. Once rebuilt the church was named after St. John the Evangelist.

The building of the Minster we see today was begun in 1220 and carried on almost continuously for 200 years, apart from a break of 50 years after the Black Death of 1349, to be completed in 1420. Many people consider it to be one of the finest examples of Gothic architecture in this country, or indeed in Europe.

Stone for the building of the Minster was brought from the West Riding of Yorkshire. It was carried down the Humber and then up the River Hull. The stream which runs from the River Hull to Beverley, the Beck, was widened and deepened to allow barges to come right up to the town and a quay was built a mile from the site of the Minster.

Beverley, which now had direct access to the sea, developed on two counts: a religious centre and a commercial centre.

Beverley as a Religious Centre

In 1201, Lady Sybil de Valoignes gave the Manor of Holy Trinity (on the site of the present railway station) to the Order of St. John of Jerusalem — the Knights Hospitallers. They provided lodging and food for the many pilgrims and travellers who visited the town.

In the fourteenth century a friary was built near the Minster. This was the house of the Black Friars who were scholars and preachers and who lived by begging for alms. They also provided accommodation for visitors. One such visitor was Edward I who, in 1299 and 1309, spent three days at the friary on his way north to fight the Scots.

Another friary was sited in what was Greyfriars Lane, but this no longer exists.

The whole area around the Minster supplied houses for the many wealthy members of the church who lived in the town. The provost of the Minster was considered to be one of the richest men in Yorkshire.

Two more churches were built — St. Nicholas Church, which became neglected after the reformation

The Friary – originally home of the Black Friars; now a Youth Hostel.

and the stones of which were later used to repair or build other churches, and St. Mary's Church.

St. Mary's Church was the church belonging to the town and it is evidence of the wealth of some of the merchants that they were able to raise the money to erect such a beautiful church. The greater part of the building took place between 1300 and 1400, and it is interesting to consider how much building was going on during this time.

Each year, until the reformation, at the festival of Corpus Christi, the Thursday after Trinity, there was a grand procession through the town. The Mystery Plays would be enacted on carts stationed at positions in the town and each craft, or guild, would be expected to re-enact a scene from the Bible. Unfortunately the script of Beverley's Mystery Plays no longer exists.

In 1423, the Earl and Countess of Northumberland came from their castle at Leconfield to join the Burgesses of Beverley on stands erected at North Bar and watch the plays.

Beverley as a Commercial Centre

A Poll Tax taken in 1377 suggested that Beverley had a population of about 5,000 and was the eleventh largest town in England.

With its religious importance, and the many visitors who came to worship at the shrine of St. John, with its easy access to the sea via the then navigable Beverley Beck, River Hull and the Humber, and with the prosperous farming land around, Beverley indeed became a wealthy town which kings and pilgrims liked to visit for both business and pleasure.

Various charters were granted to the town entitling it to certain rights and privileges, among them the right to hold a market on Saturdays and Wednesdays.

A ditch was dug around the town to set a boundary for tax purposes rather than for defence, and the five points of entry through the town gates, or Bars, ensured that the owners of carts entering the town had to pay taxes.

One of the principal trades of medieval Beverley was the cloth trade. In 1236 the cloths of Beverley were so well known that Henry III ordered some. The name of the inn in Westwood Road — the Woolpack Inn — is a reminder of those days, as are some of the street names — Walkergate, where the cloth was walked through the water to wash it; Dyer Lane; and Flemingate, a reminder of trade with the continent.

In 1380 the Archbishop of York gave the 600 acres of the Westwood to the town at an annual rent of £5. This land for many centuries provided the people of Beverley with firewood, timber for building houses and ships and free grazing rights for the freemen of the town.

Decline in the Fortunes of Beverley

However, the fortunes of the town were to change. In

the fifteenth century the wool trade declined and with it the wealth of the town. Many houses fell into disrepair and Beverley's importance remained with its religious rather than its commercial activities.

But in the sixteenth century Henry VIII decided to break with the church in Rome and take over much of the wealth of the English church for himself.

The Pilgrimage of Grace

On Sunday, 8th October 1536, following similar uprisings in Lincolnshire, the town bell of Beverley was rung in Saturday Market summoning inhabitants of the town to join in a protest at Henry's threatened dissolution of religious buildings.

On the following day, between four and five hundred men marched to the Westwood to voice their protest, and from there the rebellion spread to other parts of the north of England. But these rebellions, known as the Pilgrimage of Grace, were soon suppressed by the King's troops and many people were hanged.

The uprisings did nothing to stop Henry in his determination to plunder the wealth of the church and the majority of the buildings in Beverley associated with the church were destroyed. Four years later Beverley also lost its right of sanctuary.

It has been estimated that about one in four of the population of approximately 5,000 people in Beverley would have been concerned with the church. Many of those people would have become "unemployed" when the churches and other religious buildings were destroyed or fell into disuse.

The Minster remained intact as it was a parish church.

The Civil War

One hundred years later, Beverley was again involved in national events and during the Civil War King Charles I stayed in the town on two occasions.

At the outbreak of hostilities between king and parliament, Sir John Hotham, who represented Beverley in Parliament, was commissioned by the Roundheads to protect the arsenal in Hull and to prevent King Charles from getting hold of any arms.

However, Sir John eventually decided to support the king rather than the government and on 8th June 1643 he escaped from Hull. Finding routes to his house at Scorborough closed, he was forced to ride through Beverley. He rode into the Market Place, only to be confronted by a troop of parliamentary soldiers. Quickly he pretended to lead the troop, but to no avail as he was recognised and on trying to escape down one of the narrow alleyways leading from the Market Place he was dragged from his horse by one of Cromwell's soldiers. He and his son were then taken to Hull and from there by sea to the Tower of London where they were later beheaded.

We are told that during the Civil War there was vicious and bloody fighting in and around Beverley and much of the town was plundered. The medieval glass in St. Mary's Church was destroyed, together with all the ancient books.

The Plague in Beverley

During the seventeenth century the plague struck the town four times and many people died. Efforts were made to control the disease. Meetings of more than ten people were forbidden, contact with other towns was restricted and bales of cloth from London, feared to be carriers of the disease, were banned from the town. But the disease still worked its way through and a burial plague pit was dug on the site of the present railway station.

There were few thoughts of hygiene and streams running through the streets would have provided a deposit for refuse as well as serving as a water supply.

The houses were mostly half-timbered and small. A typical shop would have a small room at the front, a living room behind, and sleeping quarters above under a thatched roof.

Improvements in the Fortunes of the Town

Towards the end of the seventeenth century the fortunes of the town began to improve.

Edmund Gibson, visiting Beverley in 1695, writes: "The inhabitants of Beverley pay no Toll or Custom in any port or town of England; to which immunity (I suppose) they owe in a great measure their riches and flourishing condition. For indeed, one is surprised to find so large and handsome a town within six miles of Hull. The town is above a mile in length, being of late much improved in its buildings; and has pleasant springs running quite through it. The principal trade of the town is making Malt, Oat-meal and Tanned leather, but the poor people mostly support themselves by working of Bone-lace, which of late has met with particular encouragement, the children being maintained at school, to learn to read, and to work this sort of lace. The Cloath-trade was formerly followed in this town but has decayed ... They have several Fairs; one more especially remarkable, beginning about nine days before Ascension-day and kept in a street leading to the Minster called Londoner street (now Highgate). For then the Londoners bring down their wares, and furnish the Country-Tradesmen by Whole-sale."

New brick buildings were built and often several small houses would be knocked down and a large brick house built instead, perhaps as a town house for a wealthy farmer, doctor, lawyer or banker.

The roofs of these new houses would be covered with pantiles, first brought over as ballast in ships from Holland and later manufactured locally.

A pride in the town began to develop and during the

eighteenth and nineteenth centuries many improvements were made and Beverley changed its image; from being a commercial town it became a fashionable town.

Trade was improving, wealth increasing and the pursuit of leisure activities was being developed. In 1788 a theatre was built in Wood Lane and for two months of the year the Butler family from Richmond would come and play to packed houses. Assembly Rooms were built in Norwood and these were the scene of many grand dances and gatherings. Both these buildings have since been demolished. The race course was moved to its present site on the Westwood in 1769 and the race meetings became a popular event.

Civic pride developed. In 1762 the Town Council decided to improve the Guild House in Register Square; the pillared porch was added in the following century. The Guildhall, which is also the Tourist Office, is open on Tuesdays and Bank Holidays during the summer months and is well worth visiting. Guides will show you round this ancient building, which has been altered and adapted to meet the needs of the various centuries. The Courtroom with its stucco ceiling is exceptionally fine.

In the late seventeenth century Beverley became the administrative centre of the East Riding of Yorkshire and in 1892 it became the County Town of the East Riding.

Industries of Beverley

Because of the many streams running through Beverley, tanning had been a thriving industry since the fourteenth century. In 1812 William Hodgson rented premises and by the end of the nineteenth century his firm employed 450 people. In 1920 the firm was bought by Barrow Hepburn, but unfortunately trade declined and the tannery was finally closed in 1978.

In 1799 William Crosskill was born in Butcher Row. When William was just over twelve years of age his father died and he inherited the family tinsmith business. William built up the ironworks and it became so successful that it was moved to Mill Lane. Part of the success was due to the improved communications to and from Beverley which resulted from the building of the railway in 1846. During the Crimean War of 1854 Crosskill's business boomed as the firm supplied shells and carts to the army. At its height, the ironworks employed 800 people, a large number for those days. Their agricultural machinery, especially the clod-crusher, was exported all over the world. But in 1855 William Crosskill handed the firm over to his sons. It ran into financial difficulties and was finally closed in 1904.

The silting up of the Beck and the building of larger ships meant that boats could no longer sail right up to the town of Beverley. However, shipbuilding continued on the River Hull and at the end of the nineteenth century, Beverley yards were busy building ships for Hull's fishing fleets. Because the river was so narrow, ships had to be launched sideways. But the decline in the fishing industry has meant a decline in the boat building business, and little work is now carried on.

In 1913 Gordon Armstrong built a motor car and set up his garage business in North Bar Within. There he made tractors which were used on the land during the First World War. After the war he made shock-absorbers for the new motor car and business prospered.

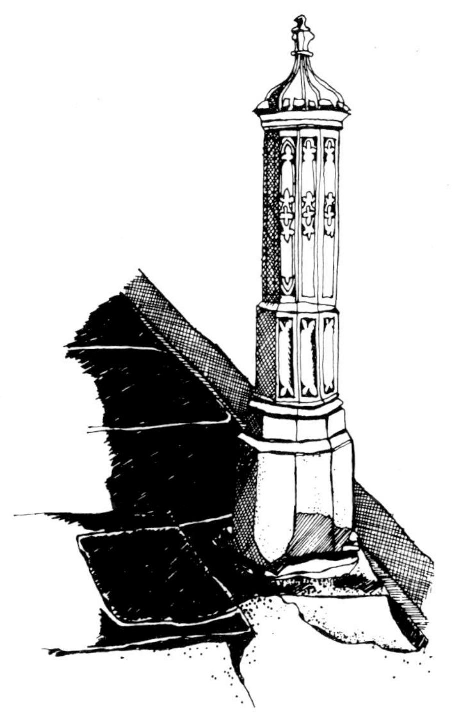

A Victorian water pump. At one time there were 900 such pumps in the town.

Improvements in the Standard of Living

During the nineteenth century, efforts were made to improve the living conditions in the town. Beverley was lit by gas light in 1824, many new schools were opened to educate the poor, a dispensary for the sick was provided and almshouses were built for the old and infirm. A new workhouse, now the Westwood Hospital, was built in 1861.

Both the Methodist religion and the evangelical movement had many followers in Beverley and John Wesley preached here on seventeen occasions. Several Methodist chapels were built.

By the beginning of the twentieth century, as a result of several outbreaks of typhoid, the open streams running through the town were covered over and a sewage system was built.

Many scenes of Beverley have been captured on canvas by Fred Elwell. He was born in the town in 1870 and after travelling on the continent settled in Beverley and for 48 years lived in the Bar House at North Bar. His vivid paintings of life in the houses and in the streets of Beverley can be seen in the Art Gallery above the Public Library.

Twentieth Century Beverley

Today the old industries have finished and new engineering and light industrial companies set up in the 1960's and 1970's have declined. The main employers are Humberside County Council (which moved here from Hull in 1984) and the Borough Council. Other employers are caravan companies and, more recently, new hi-tech concerns. Now tourism is an important industry and provider of employment and many jobs in the town are concerned with service to people — in the cafés, restaurants and shops.

Beverley remains a popular place in which to live and the majority of occupants are professional, skilled people, many of whom commute to other areas. In 1801 the population was 5,401; in 1981 it was 16,450 and by 1989 it was estimated to be 20,650. Consequently, large scale building developments have taken place and many open spaces and large gardens have been built on. Recently, many acres of land to the south of the Minster have been developed — the closeness of these developments to the Minster was a much debated subject — and many acres to the north of the town are in process of being developed.

The people of Beverley have had to recognise the needs of the changing centuries. The town has been adapted to changes in buildings, lifestyles, industries fashions and means of transport. Beverlonians of the second half of the twentieth century are proud of their town and are anxious to preserve it as a pleasant place in which to live.

It is hoped that the modern pilgrim to Beverley will agree that this is being done.

This cross was built at the expense of Sir Charles Hotham, Bart. and Sir Michael Warton, KT, members of parliament for the corporation Anno Domini 1714. Repaired 1768 William Leake Esq., Mayor.

Beverley Market Cross

A Stroll through Beverley

Let us begin our stroll where the town itself began:

The Minster

The true origin of the word 'minster' is uncertain. One explanation is that it comes from the word 'Mynster,' i.e. a church served by a group of clergy who shared a communal life and who went out as missionaries to teach Christianity to the people.

Building of the present church began in 1220 and was finished in 1430. There are many guide books available which give a detailed account of the history of this beautiful Gothic building, but places of particular interest are:

The Percy Shrine — believed to be the tomb of Eleanor Percy who died in 1328. This shrine has a beautifully carved Gothic canopy. The town of Beverley was owned by the Archbishop of York and so did not have its own castle or protector. However, the Percy family had a castle at Leconfield, two and a half miles from the town, and was considered to be the protector of the town.

The Sixteenth Century Misericords — these are carvings under the seats of the choirstalls and show many scenes from medieval life.

You will find it well worthwhile to join one of the pre-

The Frith Stool – A Saxon Sanctuary Chair which would have been the Provost's seat. There is a similar one in Hexham Abbey which also had the Right of Sanctuary.

arranged parties and climb the 114 steps up the central tower to see the treadmill which was in use until recently. If you go onto the roof of the Church you will be able to view the town and its surroundings. From this vantage point you can see the layout of the town with its winding streets, so designed to follow the course of the many streams which ran through the town, north to St. Mary's Church, the North Bar and the countryside beyond.

Today, most of the houses are built of red brick with pantile roofs, but in medieval times the scene would have been very different with timber and plaster houses with thatched roofs. Also there would have been larger buildings associated with the Minster.

Leave the Minster by the north door and turn towards the east. Go to the end of the church, cross the road and enter Friar's Lane. On the left you will find:

The Friary

This late medieval building, originally the home of the Black Friars, has recently been restored — thanks to the enthusiasm of twentieth century inhabitants of the town — and turned into a youth hostel.

Retrace your steps to the north door of the Minster and now proceed north up Highgate.

Highgate

In this street you will pass a number of elegant eighteenth and nineteenth century houses built as 'infill' into an area which was originally part of Wednesday Market.

When the plague struck the town in 1665, all dogs and cats in the area of the Minster, Highgate and

Eighteenth century houses in Highgate.

Wednesday Market were killed as they were thought to be carriers of the disease.

Note:

Number 38 (facing the Minster) — was built between 1730 and 1740. For the first 150 years it was the Blue Coat School.

Number 25 — The Monk's Walk Inn (formerly the George and Dragon). Monk's Walk is said to be the route on which victims of the plague were carried to the plague pit on the site of the present railway station.

Number 17 — note the large cornice. Gutters and drainpipes were not used until the eighteenth century so before that time houses were built with large eaves so that water from the roof was thrown away from the walls — and on to any passing pedestrians!

At the top of Highgate you will enter Wednesday Market.

Wednesday Market

Trading took place here every Wednesday from the thirteenth century until 1730 when the market was moved to the specially built cattle market. Since 1985 a market has been held here every Saturday.

Note the variety of buildings surrounding the market. Recently a fifteenth century fireplace was discovered in Number 15.

Leading off from Wednesday Market, Railway Street was built after the coming of the railway in 1846 and Lord Roberts Road, constructed in 1909, necessitated the demolition of half of Number 1 Highgate.

Proceed north and enter Butcher Row.

Butcher Row

This was where butchers sold their wares. Originally a stream ran through the centre of the street and here the butcher would slaughter his livestock and throw the offal in the stream which would then carry it down to the Beverley Beck.

Butcher Row leads into:

Toll Gavel

So named as tolls were collected here.

As you walk up the street, note the snakes curled round the pillars of a shop on the left. The snake is a

"Ye Olde Pork Shoppe" in Butcher Row. Typical of the early style of shop with living quarters behind and sleeping quarters above.

symbol of Aesculapius, the God of Medicine; thus this would have been a chemist's shop.

At the top of Toll Gavel you will enter Saturday Market.

Saturday Market

So called because for the last 700 years a market has been held here every Saturday. The pubs of Beverley have a special dispensation to remain open during the hours of market trading.

As the Minster represented the religious centre of the town, so Saturday Market represented the commercial centre.

For many centuries the market has been the centre of activities in Beverley, reflecting the feelings and ideas of the time. During the fourteenth century, when, thanks partly to its cloth industry, Beverley was a thriving and wealthy market town, visiting tradesmen, fairs and bear baiting must all have added to the bustle and excitement of the market place.

Evidence of the centuries may be seen in the buildings surrounding the Market, and the different styles of architecture reflect the fashion of the day. In many houses, if the eighteenth or nineteenth century façade were removed, an older building would be revealed. Nearly all the older shops have been replaced by 'modern' Georgian or Victorian buildings, reflecting the elegance of the eighteenth and nineteenth centuries. Now Beverley is a popular shopping centre and during the last few years multi-stores have moved in and bought up shops in the centre of the town so that the whole character of the market square is changing and the small shop keeper is unable to compete with the larger stores. Soon we will be unable to buy oranges in the market place! Seventeenth and eighteenth century interiors have been ripped out and exteriors have been altered. We must hope that the twentieth century developer will be able to maintain the attractiveness of the market place.

Crossing the Market Square, observe the Market Cross ahead. Walk past the Corn Exchange (Picture Playhouse) and enter Ladygate.

The Corn Exchange – built in 1886. In 1911 it was rented out and for 6d, 4d, or 2d, the public could enjoy a new form of entertainment – the film. Now renamed the Picture Playhouse, it is little changed inside and is a popular place where Beverlonians can see the latest film.

Ladygate

Note the old shops on the right hand side recently saved from demolition.

Proceed up the street and note on the left, the Public Baths built in late Victorian times — a necessity once people became aware of the importance of hygiene and the lack of washing facilities in most houses.

Walk up Ladygate until you reach Hengate.

Hengate

Cross over the road to St. Mary's Church and read the sad story of the two Danish soldiers in 1689, recorded on the plaque on the side of the church.

One thing which hasn't changed in the course of thirteen centuries is the position of the sun! The better houses would be built on the north side of the street so as to face the sun. Individual owners were allowed to raise the roadway, presumably to cover the streams which ran outside their door. If the causeway was raised, houses on the other side of the street could become too low and thus lose their value. This happened in Hengate.

Note:

The War Memorial — in memory of the 500 young men of Beverley who were killed in the First World War.

Number 3 — built in 1778.

Number 7 — in 1709 Henry Spendlove bought

Ladygate – with a view of St. Mary's Church.

and demolished three cottages and a house and then built the present house.

Number 16 — former Arden's Vaults. There was an early eighteenth century granary above the vaults.

The White Horse Inn — further up the street on the right hand side. This inn is known to the locals as "Nellie's", named after Nellie Collinson who retired in 1976. The pub dates from the fifteenth century and was at one time a coaching inn. In 1888 Mr. Francis Collinson became the tenant and he, his wife and their children — William, Frank, Arthur, Tim, John, David, Thomas, Lily, Nellie, Dorothy, Edith, Annie and Ada — were the licensees here for 88 years.

Now retrace your steps to St. Mary's Church.

St. Mary's Church

Note the sixteenth century tower, built to replace the tower which collapsed on Sunday, 29th April 1520, killing several members of the congregation in the church. The nave also dates from this period.

The floor of the church is well below the level of the street, another reminder that while houses are built, demolished and rebuilt over the centuries, yet the church has remained the same.

There are many guide books which give a detailed description of this lovely church, built through the generosity of the wealthy men of Beverley. The pillars on the north east of the nave have carvings of benefactors, each holding a scroll which records their gifts.

Many interesting artifacts of medieval Beverley are preserved in the Priest's Room at the east end of the church.

Re-enter the street into North Bar Within.

North Bar Within

Opposite the church is:

The Beverley Arms Hotel. Previously "The Blue Bell Inn" it was modernised in the eighteenth century in the Georgian style, and renamed. The hotel was a posting house where horses could be changed; horses which had travelled along the newly improved turnpike roads linking Beverley with Hull, the East Coast and York. It would also have been an important meeting place, where businessmen or farmers could meet and many commercial deals would have been transacted here.

It is believed that Dick Turpin, the infamous highwayman, stayed here when called before the Beverley Magistrates in 1738. In 1868, Anthony

A carving of a rabbit on a doorway in the north trancept of St. Mary's Church. Lewis Carroll used this carving as a model for his white rabbit in Alice in Wonderland.

Trollope stayed during his unsuccessful attempt to be elected as Liberal candidate for Beverley.

It was also the scene of many general elections. Beverley had, along with many other constituencies, earned a name for corrupt elections. In the by-election of 1860, Tory followers had rounded up Liberal supporters who were intoxicated, and taken them to a room in Vicar Lane. Here the Liberals had been "sobered up" with tea. In actual fact, the teapot contained laudanum and rum, leaving the Liberals in no fit state to cast their vote!

Investigations after the 1868 elections shows that 604 Beverlonians had bribed voters or been bribed. Four years later, the Secret Ballot Act was passed in order to stop corruption in elections.

Proceed up the road towards North Bar.

Note:
St. Mary's Manor (on the right) — a handsome nineteenth century alteration was made to the previous house.
On the opposite side of the road (the west side) is a timber framed house. This is one of the oldest buildings in the town, built in the fifteenth century. It was here that Gordon Armstrong opened his garage in 1908. Now it is the entrance to an example of twentieth century development, St. Mary's Arcade.

The Beverley Arms Hotel, formerly The Blue Bell Inn.

Continuing past St. Mary's Arcade:

The Tower House — this house had a tower added to it to enable the owner to watch his horses on the racecourse.

The Bar House (attached to the west side of the North Bar) is believed to be where Charles I stayed on his visits to Beverley. The present building was much altered in the eighteenth century. This was the home of Fred Elwell, the painter, for over 48 years.

North Bar

Built in 1409, for a cost of £96.0.11½d, this gateway is an example of early brickwork. Originally there were five such entries into the town, but the others have now been demolished. They were important as a means of ensuring that all drivers of carts paid their tolls on entering the town, and during outbreaks of plague, the gates would be closed to prevent anyone entering or leaving the town.

Passing through the Bar you will enter North Bar Without.

North Bar Without

Previously, to the left of the Bar, was one of the two leper houses of the town, and also the ducking pond in which gossiping women would be submerged!

At the end of the eighteenth century, the Town Council decided to provide a more civilised urban environment. Between 1778-80, North Bar Without and New Walk were planned. A wide street, along which inhabitants of the town could promenade, was designed to run north from the Bar, with suitably grand buildings on either side. A row of chestnut trees was planted in 1823 and the elegant North Bar Without was created. Here, the gentry would walk, discussing the problems and pleasures of the day. No doubt part of their discussion would be why Hull was overtaking Beverley as an important commercial centre, and the effect the coming of the railway in 1846 would have on the town.

Return to the Bar.

If you are feeling energetic, you can turn right and within a few hundred yards you will come to the area of common land known as the Westwood. Note the boards on the left hand side which describe the rules and regulations for those using the Westwood in 1836.

The Westwood — a place of bluebells, buttercups, skylarks, grazing cattle and a favourite area for twentieth century leisure pursuits such as golf, walking, sledging, horse riding. The Westwood is much used by Beverlonians and people from surrounding districts.

If, however, you do not feel energetic, why not go to one of the many cafés or pubs available and, as many other travellers throughout the centuries have done, reflect upon the history of this ancient town.

An elegant walkway – North Bar Without. The lamp-posts came from William Crosskill's factory.

Terrace of five houses in North Bar Within. They were built in the late eighteenth century with Adam style doorways and wrought iron handrails.

The Author acknowledges use of the following sources in the preparation of this book:

A Beverley Chronology	Humberside Libraries and Amenities
Historic Beverley	Ivan and Elizabeth Hall (William Sessions, 1973)
Sanctuary. Beverley — A Town of Refuge	Martin Kirby (Highgate Publications, 1986)
Beverley	K. A. MacMahon (Dalesman, 1973)
The Beverley Arms — The Story of a Hotel	John Markham (Highgate Publications, 1986)
Beverley — Official Guide	The East Yorkshire Borough of Beverley
Six More English Towns	Alec Clifton-Taylor (BBC Publications, 1981)
Old Beverley	Philip Brown (East Yorkshire History Society in association with Humberside Leisure Services, 1983)
Beverley — An Archaeological and Architectural Study	Royal Commission on Historical Monuments (HMSO, 1982)

Beverley Borough Council Planning Department

Front cover photograph by Simsons of Beverley